small group study

Rocking Ordinary Leader Guide

Holding It Together with Extraordinary Grace

Lea Ann Garfias

New Leaf Press
A Division of New Leaf Publishing Group
www.newleafpress.net

First printing: August 2016

New Leaf Press, P.O. Box 726, Green Forest, AR 72638

New Leaf Press is a division of the New Leaf Publishing Group, Inc.

ISBN: 978-0-89221-748-9

Unless otherwise noted, Scripture quotations are from the New King James Version of the Bible.

Please consider requesting that a copy of this volume be purchased by your local library system.

Printed in the United States of America

Please visit our website for other great titles:
www.newleafpress.net

For information regarding author interviews,
please contact the publicity department at (870) 438-5288

New Leaf Press
A Division of New Leaf Publishing Group
www.newleafpress.net

Introduction

How to Meet the Needs of Your Group

You are about to start an extraordinary ministry: offering hope and healing to your group of friends. Each week of this study, you will face women who are hurting, women who are discouraged, women who are weary, and each lesson you will reach out to them with God's promise of strength and renewal and victory. You will watch God change their minds, change their spirits, and change their lives. You are doing Jesus' work.

Maybe you are in need of Jesus, yourself. Perhaps you, too, are tired and burdened and scarred and scared. I know I am right now, just while I'm writing to you. I'm exhausted and worried and hurting, pleading with God for healing and hope for myself and for those I love. But you know what God has been teaching me through the journey of *Rocking Ordinary*? God is showing me that *He does extraordinary work through ordinary women . . . every single day.*

This ministry of hope and healing requires great faith on our part — faith that God is powerful, faith that we will see Him face-to-face, faith that God is keeping us in His omnipotent power until then, faith that the struggles we face now are part of His purpose for our lives, faith that our endurance to the end will radiate His glory now and for eternity. That's a huge, heaping pile of faith that we are still working to stockpile. Yet it's the entire purpose of our salvation! Just read 1 Peter 1:3–9.

I wanted to take a minute right here before you get started with this study to remind you that yes, God will change you through His Word during this study. The entire purpose of *Rocking Ordinary* is to examine the ordinary of our lives, those places we try to hide or cover up because they are boring or broken and we think God isn't using them. But He is. So while you're leading this study, don't shy away from those uncomfortable parts. Lean into them. Let the Holy Spirit open up some of those scars and cleanse the impurities and untruths that have covered them over. Be brave enough to admit your own need to God, to yourself, and to those you are teaching. Have the courage Paul displayed in Romans 7 to admit your struggles with the sin nature even while you're trying to teach these holy lessons. Then you can boldly rejoice with the Apostle in Romans chapter 8 at Christ's sanctifying power in our lives.

Remember, the women gathering with you in this study are bringing great burdens with them: the burdens of family, work, ministry, and relationships. The trials of illness, bills, death, and loneliness. The pain of abuse, neglect, addiction, and sin. You may know some of the issues that your friends are facing, but doubtless there will be hidden hurts in your group that these discussions will bring to light. As a facilitator, you will be the one they likely come to for help and counsel. And sometimes a situation may come up during discussion that catches you by surprise. To help you meet the needs of these women, here are some suggestions:

Provide resources to get help. Before beginning this study, identify experienced biblical counselors in your church and community that you can recommend. Gather names of women experienced in helping women overcome anxiety, addiction, marital problems, parenting difficulties, abuse, and other stresses. While you should absolutely pray and encourage your friends toward healing, don't attempt long-term counseling for major traumas without proper training, experience, and support.

Prepare for each week's lesson. I tried really hard to make this study easy for you, but you still should look at each lesson ahead of time. Spend some time reading *Rocking Ordinary* and highlight passages you think will be meaningful for your group. Look over the Scripture passages I suggest for discussion, and add verses that are meaningful to you and that meet your friends' specific needs. To help your group open up, share personal examples from your own life and ways that God is working in you.

Provide copies of the book. Each member of your group will get more out of this study if she personally reads *Rocking Ordinary*. Remind the group each week what chapters will be covered in the next lesson so they can each read ahead. Encourage them to think through the questions at the end of the chapter and to come prepared with thoughts on the topic. This way, your discussion will be rich and insightful with perspectives from a variety of members.

Protect your friends' privacy. During discussion time and prayer time, you may have a couple of "over-sharers." You know them — the ones who air their laundry and confess their sins publicly with sackcloth and ashes. While we want to encourage transparency and genuine encouragement, we don't want to set up a situation for gossip, slander, or humiliation. So help keep the conversation positive by bringing the discussion back to *God's working in our lives* and *the timeless truths of Scripture*. Keep the talkative friends from accidentally monopolizing the lesson by drawing out the quieter ladies. And if a hurting woman bears her soul, gently remind the group to keep the prayer request confidential and help the hurting one find a safe person to confide in.

Pray for change. God wants to use you — and every member of your study group — to make an extraordinary difference in the lives of others. That means God will change your life, the lives of your friends, and then the lives of those around you. It's an amazing ripple of glory spreading forth God's grace and love, and it all starts when He touches us personally. Depend on that relationship, that most important intimacy in your life, then magnify the power of prayer as you come together as a group.

How to Use This Study

This study is designed for a variety of uses — Sunday school class, ladies' fellowship studies, book clubs, discipleship groups, or just a group of friends around the kitchen table. Use the lessons however your group best benefits.

The lessons are broken into 4 large lessons or 8 mini-lessons. If you are using the mini-lessons, you may want to spend 30–60 minutes together on the material.

- ☐ Members read the chapter(s) ahead of time.
- ☐ At the meeting, watch the DVD presentation together.
- ☐ The facilitator guides the discussion with the given questions and/or Scriptures.
- ☐ The group discusses the point and encourages one another in the Lord.
- ☐ Take some prayer requests and pray together.
- ☐ Close with some ideas how to implement what you've learned.

For longer lessons of 90 minutes or more, combine two mini lessons (example, 1A and 1B).

- ☐ Give the group the reading assignments for both mini lessons.
- ☐ Come together and watch the first DVD presentation and follow the discussion for that section.
- ☐ Move on to the next mini lesson DVD presentation and continue with that discussion.
- ☐ Take prayer requests and pray together.
- ☐ Close with ideas on how to implement what you've learned.

With the discussion questions, allow your group to spend time sharing personal testimonies, observances from the reading, or Scripture verses that encourage their walk with the Lord. I have provided some *truths* to help you guide the group toward right thinking and new awareness of their influence, in case it's not immediately apparent to the group. Also, don't feel obligated to hash out every question given. Be sensitive toward how the Holy Spirit is guiding your group's conversation and meeting the needs of your friends through the study.

Encourage your group to come prepared to minister with one another. They may want to bring their Bible, their copy of *Rocking Ordinary*, a journal and pen, and a warm beverage. Most of all, pray for willing hearts. I'm praying with you that God touches each one, encouraging women toward extraordinary service in the midst of ordinary lives.

—Lea Ann

Part 1
Success and Failure

1A. Intro, Run with Patience (introduction and ch. 1)

After welcoming everyone, begin video 1A Intro, Run with Patience (introduction and ch. 1).

Bible passage — Hebrews 12:1–3:
Read the following biblical passage prior to the group discussion.

> *Therefore we also, since we are surrounded by so great a cloud of witnesses, let us lay aside every weight, and the sin which so easily ensnares us, and let us run with endurance the race that is set before us, looking unto Jesus, the author and finisher of our faith, who for the joy that was set before Him endured the cross, despising the shame, and has sat down at the right hand of the throne of God. For consider Him who endured such hostility from sinners against Himself, lest you become weary and discouraged in your souls.*

Discussion Questions Use these questions or any others relevant to your group to stimulate discussion:

1. Are you succeeding, or merely surviving?

   From the book:

   How do we shine forth the image of God, powerfully reflecting His presence and His purpose in our lives? How does this ordinary, everyday life create extraordinary changes in our homes, our churches, our communities?

   This is true success. And that's what I want to achieve for myself, for my daughter, for my neighbor, and for you, friend. I believe that God who called us to glorify Himself will do it through us (1 Thessalonians 5:24). We can, indeed, rock our ordinary lives when we reach out and change our world, one ordinary day at a time.

1 Thessalonians 5:24 — *He who calls you is faithful, who also will do it.*

Truth — What we may feel like is failure is, in reality, the evidence of God's working through us.

Notes: ______________________________

____

2. What is success? How do you know you are being successful or failing?

   From the book:

   We can be successful. We can be influential. We can change our world if we do just that — live and say His truths no matter the consequences, no matter the obstacles. We can see God use our ordinary lives in extraordinary ways if we have the courage and the faith to simply obey wherever we are.

   Truth — We need God's perspective on our lives. He is not interested in our performance or appearance. He wants a personal relationship with each of us.

Notes: ______________________________

____

3. How does redefining success help you keep running your race?

   Truth — When we look to Jesus (not at the circumstances around us or our failures or our friend's achievements), we can continue running with patience . . . and maybe even joy.

Notes: ______________________________

____

4. How does redefining success help you reach out to those around you?
   From the book:

   We have so many differences in our races. Where we live, whether we work, our finances, our health, our family size, our ministries, our extended community — so many factors make the race completely altered for each one of us.

   The truth is, though, that we are all in it, we are all running it at the same time, and we are all commanded to continue moving forward with patience.

   We aren't looking at each other, except for encouragement. Never comparison. We are looking to the finish line, to Christ who started it all and will hand out our finisher medal at the end. He ran it ahead of us, and we will enjoy the celebration with Him at the end.

   Truth — Our purpose and meaning and significance are realized in our relationship with Christ, and that enables us to demonstrate hope and healing toward those around us.

   God is using each of us in His own plan for His own glory.

Notes:

If this study is being done in four sessions, skip page 11 and begin at page 12. Otherwise, continue to page 11.

Prayer Time: Take prayer requests from the group, then lead in prayer. The following is a sample prayer outline, if helpful.

- ☐ Thank God for His salvation, His omnipotence, His love, and His grace.
- ☐ Pray that the message of the book, the hope and healing of Christ, becomes personal to each one there.
- ☐ Pray for personal surrender to God's perfect plan for each life represented in the group.
- ☐ Pray for some of the specific needs mentioned.
- ☐ Give a moment of silent time for private prayer.
- ☐ Praise God for His provisions and for His Word.
- ☐ Ask for God's presence and power to be real to each one as she serves God throughout the week.
- ☐ Amen!

How to Rock it This Week

Read for the next lesson chapters 2 and 3 of *Rocking Ordinary.*

Ask your group for ideas how they will put the lesson into practice this week. Be specific!

Additional ideas:

- ☐ Memorize Hebrews 12:1–3 and meditate on this truth daily.
- ☐ Keep a list of ways God is blessing your work — evidence of answered prayers, renewed relationships, spiritual growth, unexpected blessings.
- ☐ Write a thank-you note to a woman who encourages your spiritual walk.

1B. Do Not Be Afraid, Reach Out (ch. 2, 3)

Let's move on and watch video 1B now, Do Not Be Afraid, Reach Out (chs. 2, 3).

Bible Passage — John 15:11–14:
Read the following biblical passage prior to the group discussion.

> *These things I have spoken to you, that My joy may remain in you, and that your joy may be full. This is My commandment, that you love one another as I have loved you. Greater love has no one than this, than to lay down one's life for his friends. You are My friends if you do whatever I command you.*

Discussion Questions Use these questions or any others relevant to your group to stimulate discussion:

1. How does criticizing ourselves inwardly contribute to a critical attitude toward others?

   Truth — When we live in the light of God's grace and love, we are better equipped to extend the same toward those around us.

Notes:

2. Why do we assume others are criticizing us more than we are? How can we avoid being overly-sensitive?

   From the book:

   It is far too easy to deny those around us the grace we ourselves desperately need. . . . Criticism comes naturally to most people; it's an outgrowth of our own prideful sin nature. It takes conscious effort to be graceful, truly loving, and forgiving to those around us.

   Truth — Christ-like love is forgiving, kind, and inclusive. It's the love that led Jesus to the Cross for us. It's the love that compels us to reach out toward others.

Notes:

3. How can we reach out in love toward the unkind, critical, or cruel people around us?

   From the book:

   The meaner and more vicious the friend appears, the more convinced I am of the severity of her wounds. Trapped between a rock and a hard place, she lashes out in fear and desperation.

   Truth — Those around us need to be willing to change and receptive of our love for genuine healing. When they are, we can have a tremendous ministry of hope toward them.

Notes:

4. How big a priority should we make friendships? Is it really that important? Why?

   From the book:

   God works His love into my life, through my life, out of my life. He reaches out of Himself to love me, shape me, grace me with His likeness, and I reflect Him by doing the same, reaching outside my four walls toward others. God's love sees through my eyes the needs, reaches through my hands toward the needy.

   Thus, the shining badge of faith becomes loving friendship. "A new commandment I give to you, that you love one another; as I have loved you, that you also love one another. By this all will know that you are My disciples, if you have love for one another" (John 13:34–35).

   Truth — We are commanded to love one another, and that love must include active friendships.

Notes: ____

____

Part 1 – Success and Failure wrap up.

Prayer Time

Take prayer requests from the group, then lead in prayer. The following is a sample prayer outline, if helpful.

- ☐ Thank God for His love toward us on the Cross and through our daily lives.
- ☐ Pray that the message of the book, Christ's unconditional love toward us, becomes personal to each one there.
- ☐ Pray for renewed dedication toward nurturing, healing friendships.
- ☐ Pray for some of the specific needs mentioned.
- ☐ Give a moment of silent time for private prayer.
- ☐ Ask for God's love and grace to be real to each one as she serves God throughout the week.
- ☐ Amen!

How to Rock it This Week

Read for the next lesson chapter 4 of *Rocking Ordinary* (if completing 2A and 2B together, read chapters 4–6).

Ask your group for ideas on how they will put the lesson into practice this week. Be specific!

Additional ideas:

- ☐ Memorize John 15:11–14, and meditate on this truth daily
- ☐ Compile a list of "in real life" friends, and schedule dates to spend time with each one.
- ☐ Find an acquaintance at church or in your community and intentionally develop a deeper relationship.

Part 2
The Important People

2A. The Most Important Part (ch. 4)

After welcoming everyone, begin video 2A, The Most Important Part (ch. 4).

Bible Passage — Psalm 119:145–149:
Read the following biblical passage prior to the group discussion.

I cry out with my whole heart;
Hear me, O LORD!
I will keep Your statutes.
I cry out to You;
Save me, and I will keep Your testimonies.
I rise before the dawning of the morning,
And cry for help;
I hope in Your word.
My eyes are awake through the night watches,
That I may meditate on Your word.
Hear my voice according to Your lovingkindness;
O LORD, revive me according to Your justice.

Discussion Questions Use these questions or any others relevant to your group to stimulate discussion:

1. Is your devotional life characterized by craving or by condemnation? What does that reveal about our focus?

   From the book:

   Because of His sacrifice, the condemnation is gone! This is our new life — a new relationship that transcends our condemnation, our depression, our guilt, our desperate grasping and striving, the ever-present distractions of this harried existence. God's love calls us to back to that sacred relationship, to the power and peace only He can give.

   Truth — When our focus remains on Christ instead of ourselves, our relationship is strengthened.

Notes: ______________________________

____

2. What would your day look like if you craved God more than anything else? How would that change your "to do" list, your relationships, your reactions?

   Truth — Our desperation for attention, love, acceptance, provision, security, and forgiveness is only met in this intimate relationship with Christ.

Notes: ______________________________

____

3. What is the difference between what we usually call “doing our devotions” and this craving for a personal intimacy with God?

   Truth — A personal relationship with God is the difference between duty and intimacy.

Notes:

4. What changes can we make in our daily disciplines to encourage deeper intimacy with God?

   Truth — When we crave intimacy with Christ, God meets our deepest needs.

   I love those who love me, and those who seek me diligently will find me (Proverbs 8:17).

Notes:

If this study is being done in four sessions, skip page 19 and begin at page 20. Otherwise, continue to page 19.

Prayer Time

Take brief requests from the group then lead in prayer.

- ☐ Thank God for His Self, His sovereignty, His presence, and His love.
- ☐ Pray that the message of the book, the hope and healing of Christ, becomes personal to each one there.
- ☐ Pray for growth in personal intimacy, that each member will be drawn to the heart of her Heavenly Father.
- ☐ Pray for some of the specific needs mentioned.
- ☐ Give a moment of silent time for private prayer.
- ☐ Praise God for Christ's death on the Cross that makes this relationship possible.
- ☐ Ask God to continue to draw each one to Himself, so that she knows His love personally.
- ☐ Ask for God's presence and love to be real to each one as she serves God throughout the week.
- ☐ Amen!

How to Rock it This Week

Read for the next lesson chapter 5–6 of *Rocking Ordinary*

Ask your group for ideas how they will put the lesson into practice this week. Be specific!

Additional ideas:

- ☐ Memorize Psalm 110:147–149 and meditate on this truth daily.
- ☐ Create a new discipline by setting an alarm mid-day and then spending five minutes in prayer.
- ☐ Change something about your daily devotions to create excitement about meeting God. Buy a new journal Bible, decorate a notebook for copying verses, or begin a new reading plan.

2B. Love, Leadership, and Marriage/Raising Leaders (ch. 5, 6)

Note: While this lesson focuses on marriage and parenting, the principles of influence, communication, and commitment apply to a variety of relationships. Please encourage your friends who are unmarried or childless to participate, applying the questions to their close friends and children's ministries.

Let's move on and watch video 2B now, Love, Leadership and Marriage, Raising Leaders (chs. 5, 6).

Bible Passage – Ephesians 5:1–2:
Read the following biblical passage prior to the group discussion.

Therefore be imitators of God as dear children. And walk in love, as Christ also has loved us and given Himself for us, an offering and a sacrifice to God for a sweet-smelling aroma.

Discussion Questions Use these questions or any others relevant to your group to stimulate discussion:

1. If leadership is influence, why do we struggle so to appreciate the influence we have at home?

   From the book:

   In spite of the world's clamor for women to achieve more, be more, do more, in reality *our success is directly tied to our most intimate relationship.* What we are in secret is what we are in public, and what we are in our bedroom is what we are in church. We cannot achieve more in God's economy than we are willing to sacrifice inside our own sacred home.

   Truth — Our love and service in daily life changes the relationships around us.

Notes:

2. If we re-define our leadership as intimate influence, how does that transform our marriage and family life?

   From the book:

   As women, we think of leadership as something we do *out there*, as what strangers and coworkers and church members and community members know us for. But radical, world-changing, extraordinary leadership is intimacy, and it starts with our own marriage.

   Truth — In order to genuinely love and support our spouse and children, we must be humbly willing to change ourselves.

Notes: ______________________________

____

3. How do we demonstrate to our spouse that our marriage is a priority . . . in good times and in the bad?
   Many waters cannot quench love,
   Nor can the floods drown it.
   If a man would give for love
   All the wealth of his house,
   It would be utterly despised (Song of Solomon 8:7).

   Truth — All marriages face difficulties both small and great. Our success as a couple depends on our individual humility, commitment, and passion for one another.

Notes: ______________________________

____

4. Why are honesty and transparency so critical to intimate influence with your spouse and children?
And above all things have fervent love for one another, for "love will cover a multitude of sins." Be hospitable to one another without grumbling. As each one has received a gift, minister it to one another, as good stewards of the manifold grace of God (1 Peter 4:8–10).

Truth — Sincerity and humility communicates love toward others.

Notes:

Part 2 – The Important People wrap up.

Prayer Time

Take prayer requests from the group, then lead in prayer. The following is a sample prayer outline, if helpful.

- ☐ Thank God for His love toward us on the Cross and through our daily lives.
- ☐ Pray that the message of the book, Christ's unconditional love toward us, becomes personal to each one there.
- ☐ Pray for strengthened families through sacrificial love.
- ☐ Pray for some of the specific needs mentioned.
- ☐ Give a moment of silent time for private prayer.
- ☐ Ask for God's love and grace to be real to each one as she serves God throughout the week.
- ☐ Amen!

How to Rock it This Week

Read for the next lesson chapter 7 of *Rocking Ordinary* (if completing 3A and 3B together, read chapters 7–9).

Ask your group for ideas how they will put the lesson into practice this week. Be specific!

Additional ideas:

- ☐ Memorize Ephesians 5:1–2, and meditate on this truth daily.
- ☐ Schedule a date with your spouse to discuss what you learned.
- ☐ Find an opportunity to speak with your child about his relationship with God. But don't talk too much — carefully listen for ways you can better model your faith and areas you can pray for your child.

Part 3

The Painful Parts

3A. Misshapen Homes (ch. 7)

After welcoming everyone, begin video 3A, Misshapen Homes (ch. 7).

Bible Passage — Psalm 27:13–14:
Read the following biblical passage prior to the group discussion.

I would have lost heart, unless I had believed
That I would see the goodness of the LORD
In the land of the living.
Wait on the LORD;
Be of good courage,
And He shall strengthen your heart;
Wait, I say, on the LORD!

Discussion Questions Use these questions or any others relevant to your group to stimulate discussion:

1. How can we help our friend work through the seven steps of healing outlined in this chapter?

   ☐ Recognize the lies
   ☐ Find safe friends
   ☐ Take your time
   ☐ Set protective boundaries
   ☐ Tell the truth
   ☐ Re-examine beliefs
   ☐ Cling to God

   Truth — God heals the pain as we work through these steps with a safe friend.

Notes:

2. How can we demonstrate to those around us that we are safe people? Characteristics of safe people:

   - ☐ They are characterized by love for others.
   - ☐ They not only refrain from gossip, criticism, and tale-bearing, but they avoid those who do.
   - ☐ They are loyal friends, maintaining friendships over years and miles.
   - ☐ They have a close, intimate walk with God that affects every aspect of their life.
   - ☐ They know God's healing power over their own broken past and rejoice in the new life the Lord has given them.
   - ☐ They sacrifice for their loved ones, maintaining relationships with their spouse, grown children, and childhood friends through thick and thin.
   - ☐ They take personal responsibility for their own failings, and they are quick to forgive others.
   - ☐ They never use relationships to exalt their own standing but rather seek to serve.
   - ☐ They keep close confidence, pray faithfully, and rejoice in God's care.

   Truth — These are characteristics of loving friendship we all should practice.

Notes:

3. What role does truth play in the healing process?

   From the book — Reconciliation is only possible through the truth.

   Sanctify them by Your truth. Your word is truth (John 17:17).

   Truth — God's Word is truth itself, and all healing comes from Him.

Notes: ______

______

4. How can we initiate the healing process in hurting people around us?

   Truth — God wants to use us as His image to bring hope and healing in our homes, churches, and communities.

Notes: ______

______

If this study is being done in four sessions, skip page 27 and begin at page 28. Otherwise, continue to page 27.

Prayer Time

Take prayer requests from the group, then lead in prayer. The following is a sample prayer outline, if helpful.

- ☐ Thank God for His love, grace, and mercy every morning.
- ☐ Pray that God will continue to work His healing in each life represented there.
- ☐ Pray for renewed faith through sacrificial love.
- ☐ Pray for some of the specific needs mentioned.
- ☐ Give a moment of silent time for private prayer.
- ☐ Ask for God's love and grace to be real to each one as she serves God throughout the week.
- ☐ Amen!

How to Rock it This Week

Read for the next lesson chapters 8 and 9 of *Rocking Ordinary*.

Ask your group for ideas on how they will put the lesson into practice this week. Be specific!

Additional ideas:

- ☐ Memorize your favorite verse from Psalm 27, and meditate on this truth daily.
- ☐ Speak with a counselor about a painful relationship you are struggling with.
- ☐ Share a word of encouragement and hope to a woman you know is hurting.

3B. That Painful Past/Painful People (ch. 8, 9) — 15 minutes

Let's move on and watch video 3B now, The Painful Past, Painful People (chs. 8, 9).

Bible Passage — James 1:2–5:
Read the following biblical passage prior to the group discussion.

> *My brethren, count it all joy when you fall into various trials, knowing that the testing of your faith produces patience. But let patience have its perfect work, that you may be perfect and complete, lacking nothing. If any of you lacks wisdom, let him ask of God, who gives to all liberally and without reproach, and it will be given to him.*

Discussion Questions: Use these questions or any others relevant to your group to stimulate discussion:

1. Why do you think physical and emotional trials stir up regret and guilt within us? How should we deal with that?

   Truth — God often uses painful people and painful experiences to expose our own sin.

Notes:

2. Why do we bury the dreams, the talents, the abilities that God has given us?

   Truth — Satan wants to defeat God's plan for us by using our sin and shame to discourage us. But Christ's sacrifice for us and the Holy Spirit's work within us is more powerful than any wrong we can do.

Notes: ________________________________

3. Why are we often afraid to speak up in our own defense against bullies and other painful people?

   Truth — God gave each of us spouses, friends, and church family to help us overcome evil.

Notes: ________________________________

4. How can we identify women in our church and community who are battling painful circumstances? How can we reach out to them in meaningful ways?

   Truth — God intends us to be agents of hope and healing for those around us.

Notes:

Part 3 – The Painful Parts wrap up.

Prayer Time

Take prayer requests from the group, then lead in prayer. The following is a sample prayer outline, if helpful.

- ☐ Thank God for His healing and forgiveness because of His work on the Cross.
- ☐ Pray that God will continue to work His healing in each life represented there.
- ☐ Pray for renewed faith in His divine working.
- ☐ Pray for some of the specific needs mentioned.
- ☐ Give a moment of silent time for private prayer.
- ☐ Ask for God's love and grace to be real to each one as she serves God throughout the week.
- ☐ Amen!

How to Rock it This Week

Read for the next lesson chapter 10–12 of *Rocking Ordinary* (if completing 4A and 4B together, read chapters 10–14).

Ask your group for ideas on how they will put the lesson into practice this week. Be specific!

Additional ideas:

- ☐ Memorize James 1:2–5, and meditate on this truth daily.
- ☐ Identify a pile of "laundry" in your heart's closet and get to work on it. Seek forgiveness. Work toward healing. And take the first steps toward obedience.
- ☐ Find a hurting woman near you. Listen to her heart's cry. Ask her for a specific way to help. Give her a hug. Then pray for her regularly.

Part 4
Significant Influence

4A. Leading from the Pew/Community Influence/True Compassion (ch. 10–12)

After welcoming everyone, begin video 4A, Leading From the Pew, Community Influence, True Compassion (ch. 10).

Bible Passage — 2 Corinthians 1:3–7:
Read the following biblical passage prior to the group discussion.

> *Blessed be the God and Father of our Lord Jesus Christ, the Father of mercies and God of all comfort, who comforts us in all our tribulation, that we may be able to comfort those who are in any trouble, with the comfort with which we ourselves are comforted by God. For as the sufferings of Christ abound in us, so our consolation also abounds through Christ. Now if we are afflicted, it is for your consolation and salvation, which is effective for enduring the same sufferings which we also suffer. Or if we are comforted, it is for your consolation and salvation. And our hope for you is steadfast, because we know that as you are partakers of the sufferings, so also you will partake of the consolation.*

Discussion Questions Use these questions or any others relevant to your group to stimulate discussion:

1. What kind of difference do we make in our families, our churches, and our communities with this one ordinary life?

   And let us not grow weary while doing good, for in due season we shall reap if we do not lose heart (Galatians 6:9).

   Truth — God uses us in ways we don't see now, but in eternity we will know His plan, that He is glorified in every ordinary moment.

Notes: ______________________________

____

2. How do women lead biblically in their homes and in their churches?

   Truth — God uses us leading from the pew and impacting our ministries for Him.

Notes: ______________________________

____

3. How do our packed-busy schedules diminish our influence?

   Truth — We must constantly fight to prioritize the people and relationships God has given us.

Notes:

4. How is our influence magnified by how we give and receive compassion?

   Truth — None of us are independent. We need the humility to accept help, and we need the courage to reach out.

Notes:

If this study is being done in four sessions, skip page 35 and begin at page 36. Otherwise, continue to page 35.

Prayer Time

Take prayer requests from the group, then lead in prayer. The following is a sample prayer outline, if helpful.

- ☐ Thank God for His gift of the Holy Spirit, who empowers us for His work.
- ☐ Pray that God will continue to use each member for His glory.
- ☐ Pray for renewed faith in His divine working.
- ☐ Pray for some of the specific needs mentioned.
- ☐ Give a moment of silent time for private prayer.
- ☐ Ask for God's love and grace to be real to each one as she serves God throughout the week.
- ☐ Amen!

How to Rock it This Week

Read for the next lesson the rest of *Rocking Ordinary*.

Ask your group for ideas on how they will put the lesson into practice this week. Be specific!

Additional ideas:

- ☐ Memorize 2 Corinthians 1:3–7, and meditate on this truth daily.
- ☐ Identify a church ministry or community outreach you can serve in. Get involved!
- ☐ Take a look at your schedule. Do you need to plan more "margin" in your life so you can be responsive to the needs around you?

4B. The Time Budget/Dare to Dream (ch. 13–14)

Let's move on and watch video 4B now, The Time Budget, Dare to Dream (chs. 11, 12).

Bible Passage — Jeremiah 29:11:
Read the following biblical passage prior to the group discussion.

> *I know the thoughts that I think toward you, says the LORD, thoughts of peace and not of evil, to give you a future and a hope.*

Discussion Questions: Use these questions or any others relevant to your group to stimulate discussion:

1. Are you hopelessly trying to "balance it all," or are you working a time budget instead of balance?

   Truth — There are seasons, years, months, and hours when God gives us disruptive priorities. Learning to budget our physical and emotional resources helps us follow His plan.

Notes:

2. Are you enjoying how you spend your time budget? If not, what changes should you make?

   Truth — We need regular accounting (daily, weekly, and seasonally) to intentionally spend our time.

Notes:

3. How can we envision the plan God has for our ordinary lives?

   Truth — God dreamed us before creation (Ephesians 1:4–6), and He is using us for His glory.

Notes:

4. How do you envision the perfect life now? Has that changed?

   Truth — As we grow in grace, we will become increasingly sensitive to how the Lord is using us and those around us.

Notes:

Part 4 – Significant Influence wrap up.

Prayer Time

Take prayer requests from the group, then lead in prayer. The following is a sample prayer outline, if helpful.

- ☐ Thank God for His sovereign will in each life.
- ☐ Pray that God will continue to use each member for His glory.
- ☐ Pray for renewed faith in His divine working.
- ☐ Pray for some of the specific needs mentioned.
- ☐ Give a moment of silent time for private prayer.
- ☐ Ask for God's love and grace to be real to each one as she serves God throughout the week.
- ☐ Amen!

How to Rock it This Week

Finish reading *Rocking Ordinary.*

Ask your group for ideas how they will put the lesson into practice this week. Be specific!

Additional ideas:

- ☐ Memorize Ephesians 1:4–6, and meditate on this truth daily.
- ☐ Consider how the Lord has spoken to you through this story. What changes does He want you to make?
- ☐ Reach out to another woman who needs hope and healing. Invite her to study *Rocking Ordinary* together.
- ☐ Do you have questions about any of the lessons or a testimony of how the Lord is working in your life? Contact Lea Ann personally at lagarfias.com/contact.

OPEN & GROW

Stressed Out Small Group Kit

978-0-89221-747-2 **$49.99**

Stressed Out Leaders Guide

978-0-89221-746-5 **$11.99**

Stressed Out DVD (95 min.)

713438-10233-7 **$25.99**

Stressed Out Book

978-0-89221-743-4 **$13.99**

Includes: Leader's guide, *Stressed Out: A Practical, Biblical Approach to Anxiety* book, and DVD of practical teaching by author Todd Friel. This study is designed to be done in 5 parts lasting 60-90 minutes each and will help small groups apply Biblical truths to replace fear, anxiety, and depression with peace.

New Leaf Press
A Division of New Leaf Publishing Group
www.newleafpress.net